Y

MW01502743

&

Directionless

A STORY OF OVERCOMING ADVERSITY
RECONNECTING WITH MY PURPOSE
TO PURSUE MY PASSION

REINALDO G TORRES JR

RGT MEDIA PRODUCTIONS

Copyright © 2023 by Reinaldo G Torres Jr. All Rights Reserved.
No part of this publication maybe not reproduced in any form
without the permission of the author.
All Photos are from the personal collection of Nana a.ka.
Marie Torres and may not be reproduced in any form
without permission of the author.

YOUNG, GIFTED, & DIRECTIONLESS

Young Gifted and Directionless is a work of nonfiction meant to empower and motivate the reader. The tips and lessons in this book are not a replacement for actual work, effort, and time that must be invested to build a successful business. Although this publication is designed to provide accurate information, the publisher and author assume no responsibility for inaccuracies of time and events.

Published by in the United States RGT Media Productions LLC.
Cover art: Canva
Edited: Shelley Mascia
ISBN: 979-8-218-21604-7

Acknowledgements

I would like to thank God for giving me the gift of creativity and the gift-of-gab. None of this would be possible without him.

To my mom, you gave me life. I have always told you; you deserve piles of flowers and gifts. But not even all of those can show you how much you mean to me, thank you for making my dreams your own.

To my dad, you also gave me life. From birth, you prayed for me. You have shown what it means to hit rock bottom, get back up, and keep going! You have played an important role in this creative process. Thank you for your time, your energy, and most importantly, your love.

To my grandfather George, your wisdom, your love, your strength, your determination and strong will to survive has definitely rubbed off on me. Your lessons have not gone unnoticed.

To my Nana, surprise!! I worked on this for you in secret! So, if you see some pictures out of place in some of the scrapbooks, you know why! You have been my rock through everything. You pushed me to be the best I could be even though there were moments I didn't want you to. I am glad you did. As the song goes, I am everything I am because you love me!

To my grandmother Catherine. I don't know of many great grandmothers who would walk away from their jobs, to take care of their grandson. You did! You have always encouraged me to have my own mind. Thank you for everything you have done and continue to do for me. I love you!

To my team at RGT Media Productions, thank you all for saying yes and showing up for me. I couldn't think of a better group of people to be on this journey with. I cannot wait to create the next chapter of memories with you guys!

Finally, to my grandmother Mattie. I know you are in Heaven smiling down on me. I feel your presence every day I sit down to write. There is not a day that goes by that I don't think about you. I hope I am making you proud.

PREFACE

What do you want to be when you grow up?

When I was a kid, my career goals were simple. I wanted to be a teacher. In fact, I would take my action figures, stick their arms in the handles of my dresser drawers, and stand in my room, in front of a small whiteboard and pretend I was teaching English. That was playtime for me as a kid. I thought being a teacher was a great job. It certainly made the adults in my family happy to hear me have my future decided at a young age.

Now, I think that is somewhat of an aimless question to ask a child-*What do you want to be when you grow up?* I mean sure, every parent wants to know what their child's plans are for the future. The problem is we are asked this question a million times until we are 18 as if that one career path is the only thing we are supposed to pursue. Heaven help you if you change.

Guess what? I did! I am not a teacher; I am not any of the things I said I wanted to be growing up. Instead, I am an entrepreneur. Growing up, entrepreneurship was not something that was encouraged or discussed. It certainly wasn't something you went to college to study.

But I think the spirit of entrepreneurship has always been inside of me. It certainly has been revealed to me in different ways over the last few years. The journey has challenged me, humbled me, and it has given me the courage to tell this story.

It's been suggested to me several times over the last few years that I write a book about my life. My first thought is always, "One day, maybe." Followed by, "Do I really want to do that?"

Writing about myself makes me feel a bit uncomfortable mostly because it's something I did not think I would be doing this early in my life. I always thought writing a book was something people did after having extraordinary careers.

However, as I write this, I realize I have had an extraordinary career. Full of memories and experiences, full of lessons that I am ready to share with you. Lessons that helped me reconnect with my purpose and discover a new path.

You see friends, there was a time I wanted nothing to do with a career in writing, speaking, or media. It was the career path I did everything in my power to ignore.

There was a time in my life that I was young, gifted, and directionless.

CHAPTER 1

I know a thing or two about overcoming adversity. It should have been my middle name. From the start, my life was anything but ordinary. I was born on October 27, 1990, and I suffered a massive stroke right after birth.

My mother, Tonya, was in seventh month of pregnancy. Apparently, I just could not wait to get here. The doctors told my parents shortly after my birth that my chances of survival were extremely slim.

"If he makes it, he will not be able to talk or walk." Startling words for brand new parents. Every day was a 50/50 chance that I could live or die. You can say that the odds were against me, but God and his angels sure weren't. I spent six months in the hospital. My dad came and fed me every single day.

The first few years of my life were not typical. I started walking at the age of two and that's when my family noticed there was something wrong with my right hand and leg. As it turns out, this was the beginning of a long journey of overcoming adversity.

When I was in Pre-Kindergarten, I mostly sat in the back of the classroom and would not talk to anyone. As you can imagine, this threw up all kinds of red flags. My teachers thought I had developed a learning disability due to the stroke until one day I stood up in the middle of the classroom and started to speak! Not only could I speak, but I had an incredible memory. I had beaten the odds and proven all those doctors wrong. I was a miracle baby with a village supporting him.

I grew up with a fantastic village. My great-great grandmother, Catherine Loud, raised me from a baby,

She is my mother's grandmother. She retired in 1992 as a nurse's aide to take care of me full time. Because she retired early, we didn't have a lot of money, but she did the best she could to make sure I wanted for nothing and that I was happy and healthy.

I spent weekends with my father's parents, George and Marie Torres. They were still working when I was growing up: Marie, as a schoolteacher for Miami Dade Public Schools and George as an Agricultural Inspector and of course, there was my great-great grandmother on my father's side, Mattie. My mother Tonya is a nail technician, my father Reinaldo Sr. works in construction. I am not saying this to brag but I am truly blessed.

This journey of overcoming adversity really began one weekend on summer vacation. The summer before I entered Kindergarten, my grandparents, George and Marie, brought back a children's book from their trip to Orlando. It was a Mickey and Minnie treasure hunt story with the names of my family in it.

One morning as I sat at the breakfast table with them, they noticed I am reciting the book WORD for WORD without looking at it. I remember Marie jumping up from the table and calling our next-door neighbor. The neighbor comes over and my grandmother says to me,

"Recite this over again!"

I wasn't sure what was happening but the smiles on their faces and the look of shock on my neighbor's face obviously meant something. After my neighbor left, my grandmother asked me where I learned to do that? I didn't answer because I didn't know I *could* do that.

By the end of that weekend, I had recited that book to practically everyone my grandmother knew. The attention at first was a little awkward to say the least. I was 5 years old; most 5-year-olds are having play dates with other kids or getting in activities or games; here I was reciting words from a book in front of people. Everyone was in shock. They could not believe I had this incredible memory.

Before I went back home that weekend, my grandmother found a poem called *"Be The Best of Whatever You Are,"* by Douglas Mallock. She printed it out and said, "Next weekend, when you come over, try to have the first verse memorized."

"Okay," I said to her before leaving.

By that next weekend when she picked me up, I had the entire poem memorized. I didn't know it yet, but this was the beginning of something special. Not only did I have an incredible memory, I had the gift of gab.

Word spread like wildfire that I had the gift of gab, and everyone wanted to hear me speak. They wanted to hear my story of beating the odds.

One day, several years later, one person in particular was really interested. She lived across the street from my great-grandmother Catherine. Her name was Josie Portier.

She worked as a volunteer at the City of Miami Police Department inside the Public Information Office. She had heard my story from my great- grandmother and she had some people she wanted to introduce me to, and she would be calling in the next few days. I can remember being pulled out of school early a few days later and being driven to the City of Miami Police Department with my grandmothers.

As I sat in the lobby next to Grandmother Marie, I remember asking her, "I thought I did something good?"

"You did," she replied.

"Then why am I at the police station?" I asked.

"Well, Ms. Portier wants to introduce you to a few friends of hers, " she said.

Moments later, we are in the Public Information Office and in walks Delrish Moss.

He extended his hand and automatically I knew I had a lifelong friend. After reciting the lines, he took me by the arm and introduced me to a couple of other officers he worked with. One in particular was Angel Calzadilla. Much like Delrish, we connected instantly; another lifelong friend.

You know how they say people come into your life or a reason or a season? People like Delrish, Josie, and Angel came into my life for a reason.

A couple of weeks after meeting Delrish and Angel, Ms. Portier came by and said there was one more person she wanted me to meet. Her name was Jodi Atkinson, and she was the executive director of the Do The Right Thing program, which rewards children for positive behavior and good deeds in their community.

Much like everyone else, Jodi heard about my story and asked if I could speak at one of her events coming up. My grandparents agreed and we went home.

One the day of event, I walked into the police department with both of my grandmothers and the lobby was full of people. Jodi introduced

4

me to a few people and then…Showtime! All eyes were on me as I walked to the podium. I remember the podium was taller than me and I had to stand on a box to see over it.

Here I am, giving my first speech in front of a room full of cops, and people dressed in suits, wanting to hear me speak. Talk about the longest three minutes of my life! By the end of those three minutes, the crowd erupted in a standing ovation. People were patting me on the back or pulling me in for a hug to say good job.

After the event was over, I asked my grandmother Marie, "What did they call that? What I had just done?"

"You are a motivational speaker," she said.

In the days and weeks following, it seemed like the phones were ringing off the hook with people booking me to speak at events. I was even in the newspaper. A third grader getting local recognition because of the gift to gab. Imagine if Social Media had existed back then!

Jodi called about two weeks later, to tell my family that I was in the running for a trip to England with other Do the Right Thing participants and she would notify us in the coming weeks if I won.

A trip to England? Me? I thought. This all seemed too good to be true. I remember thinking, *What was so special about me? Why was I getting all this recognition?*

My grandmother Marie explained to me. "You have a gift. There are not a lot of kids who survive the odds like you did."

If I thought my name was spreading like wildfire when I first started speaking, being notified that I was in the running for a trip to England took that to a WHOLE new level. My grandmother Marie was telling all of her co-workers about my accomplishments, and I was highly popular among some of my teachers. Without question, though, this made a lot of the other children at school jealous. I did not have many friends except for Ms. Portier's two grandchildren, Harold and Vanecia Scott, so I stayed to myself and focused on schoolwork.

On September 1st, 1999, I received my official letter from the Do The Right Thing Program notifying me that I had won the trip to England. I still could not believe this was real! I was about to travel out of the country for the first time in my life. But who would go with me? My grandmother Catherine was afraid of flying, my mom and dad were both working and my dad was afraid of flying. Therefore, Grandmother Marie took off a few days to accompany me to England.

There were nine of us. I was the smallest and youngest. One of the winners (who shall remain nameless) thought it would be fun to pick on the little guy. Every chance this guy got, he did or said things to get under my skin. I can remember his mother verbally warning of the consequences he would face if he continued to make trouble for me. I was not going to let this kid ruin my trip because this was a once in a lifetime opportunity and I was going to savor every minute of it.

We were documented by NBC 6 on the trip. This is where I received my first critical lesson in storytelling. I was being interviewed by Martha Sulgalski. This was my first time ever being interviewed for television. I was more focused on the camera in front of me than on her.

After the camera stopped rolling, she pulled me aside and said, "In the future, always keep eye contact on the person in front of you and always project your voice."

Then it hit me. For the first time since I started speaking, I was nervous. For whatever reason, this was not like my other speeches, I was going to be on TV. The world was watching me now.

CHAPTER 2

By the summer of 1999, I had finished third grade at Allapattah Elementary School (Now Lenora Braynon Smith). My grandparents received a phone call from Dr. Frederick Morley, who was the principal of Charles R. Drew Elementary School.

He called to tell them that the school was accepting applications for its magnet program, and he wanted me to audition for drama for the upcoming school year. I auditioned and I got in! This meant I would be starting fourth grade at a new school.

Adjusting to a new learning environment did not stop me. I continued to speak at several events for several different organizations; The Children's home society of Florida, The Urban League; I even became a junior master of ceremony alongside Delrish Moss for Josie Portier's Passover and Good Friday Service. This was an annual celebration that brought together local politicians, and law enforcement officers to honor them for their work in the community.

The highlight of fourth grade came that summer when I was asked to give the Innovational address at Alonzo Mourning's Summer Groove Charity Event. I was introduced by Jim Berry of CBS4. Most people would be a bundle of emotions taking pictures with celebrities and sports figures but I was just honored to participate.

I can recall getting up on that stage; this was the biggest audience I had ever addressed. Alonzo Mourning and his wife Tracey were seated at a table in the front a few feet away from me. You know that feeling of anxiety you get when you are excited or nervous about something? That moment you can hear your heart beating? Yep, that was me.

"Are you nervous?" My grandmother had asked me en route to the hotel,

"No." I responded.

This question was followed by her pep talk on my delivery: "Remember when you speak, put emphasis on your words, speak clearly, don't use fill-ins like uh and uh." She usually repeated this about a dozen times before we reached the hotel. I am the one who should be nervous right?? Anyway, I flashback to this conversation as I stand on stage. I take a deep breath and start my speech.

By the end of the event, I had taken so many pictures, I felt like I was being blinded. As we were waiting for the valet, people were lined up asking for my autograph. I really felt like a celebrity that night. I can recall signing program booklets for a few of the guests and yelling, "Next in line." That sure gave my grandmothers a laugh on the way home.

Despite all the success, there were challenges. By the time I started fifth grade that following August, I was excelling in every subject except Math. I struggled with math a lot during elementary and middle school. I had tutors, some of whom were upset at the fact that I wasn't grasping math as quickly as the other kids. They probably thought I was not going to amount to anything. It is not like I hadn't heard that before. One thing I have come to learn over the years is that people will try to undermine you and underestimate you; it is up to you to prove them wrong.

In fifth grade, I was also introduced to my new drama teacher Michelle Riu. She took me under her wing and mentored me. A monologue was our first class assignment. For whatever reason, two students in the class took an instant dislike to me and they were very vocal about it. Most of the kids in my classes that year were vocal about their dislike. I knew why, but I was determined not to let it bother me.

One day during math class, I was called down to the principal's office. I was very confused because I had never been called down to the principal's office. He had someone he wanted me to meet. I walked into his office and seated in a chair across from him is Norman Braman. Yep, Norman Braman; former owner of the Philadelphia Eagles, owner of Braman Motors in Miami.

Dr. Morley shared my story and Mr. Braman wanted to hear me speak. After reciting "Be the Best of Whatever You Are," he said that he wanted to stay in touch with me and the things I was doing. I shook his hand and went off to my next class.

After school, as I was waiting for my grandmother Catherine to pick me up, two students pinned me against a wall and started to taunt me. They didn't like me because of the attention from the other teachers and because I walked with a limp. Luckily, a teacher walked by and scared them off.

I learned later from another classmate that those two students, along with another, were planning to jump me. I told my grandmother I did not wish to return to school. Part of me was angry because I wanted to get back at them, but that was not in my nature. My grandmother Catherine on the other hand...was a different story!

For the next several weeks, she stayed outside of the school, making sure the other kids didn't harass me. She asked me to point out the students who were planning to jump me. She warned them to their faces if they laid a finger on me, the cops would be taking her to jail. The next day after that verbal warning, those kids were my best friends, walking me to class, helping me carry my books.

My homeroom teacher, Mrs. Bennet, pulled my grandmother to the side and asked, "Ms. Loud, what did you say to those kids?"

"I was not going to put my hands on them, I just warned them if they messed with my baby, the cops would be taking me to jail," she responded. To this day, she still calls me her baby and that verbal warning is still true.

Now here is an interesting plot twist. One of the students who was harassing me attended the same church. In fact, she sat three rows behind me and my grandmother. However, she never said anything to me, and I never said anything to her.

It is a funny thing about people, Monday-Saturday, they will show their true colors and act a plumb fool and treat people all kinds of wrong, but come Sunday, they are perfect angels who could do no wrong!

By the end of that school year, my grandmother Marie Torres had been retired from Miami Dade County Public Schools for just over a year. My grandfather George retired the year before her. They had heard about what happened to me at the school and decided there was no way I would be attending a public junior high school.

For the next several weeks, Marie searched high and low for private schools, but everything already been filled and I would be placed on a waiting list. Her brother-in-law Marvin Ellis told her of a private school in Miami Springs, Blessed Trinity. They had two spots open! I had to take the entrance exam that day. I passed and I would start sixth grade in a new school.

That year, I had enemies. People who were jealous of my success and they expressed it by bullying me. I could have easily fought back or spread nasty rumors about them. But I didn't. Instead, I walked away.

This experience taught me valuable lessons about adversity. The first is that bullies do not deserve one cent of my time. By fighting back and spreading rumors, I would have become part of the problem, not the solution. The biggest piece of advice I can give to anyone overcoming adversity is: Don't worry about those who talk behind your back, they are behind you for a reason. Now I know, that might be easier said than done.

In today's world, victims of bullying, not only have to worry about face-to-face harassment, but also being bullied on social media. I could not imagine being in grade school now and having to deal with that added pressure.

CHAPTER 3

Ironically, when I started sixth grade at Blessed Trinity Catholic School, I felt out of place. I was one of two African American at the school and was the only African American in my class. I was jumping to worse case scenarios in my head with every person that tried to approach me. None of that mattered because my new classmates welcomed me with open arms.

Those first few months, I didn't share many of my accomplishments with my new classmates, not because I was shy, but I just wanted to enjoy a little peace and quiet. I had just overcome all the bullying and harassment during the previous school year, and didn't want history repeating itself.

On the first day, my grandmother Marie picked me up.

"How was it?" she asked excitedly.

"It was great," I responded.

"Were kids nice to you?" she asked.

"Yes. Everything is cool," I said.

For the next few weeks, every car ride from school started the same way. After everything that happened at my last school, my family just wanted to make sure I was comfortable. Still, I kept my guard up and my head down.

I didn't do much speaking that year. I gave a speech for the 100 Black Men of Tomorrow. I was still the junior MCEE at Josie's Good

Friday service and I was invited back to Zo's Summer Groove in 2003 to give the invocational speech. It was a quiet year which felt great.

That summer, I went on a trip with my dad to Universal Studios. While walking through the park, I started complaining of pain in my feet. At first, we both thought it was just the normal fatigue that came with walking an entire theme park from sunrise to sunset.

Later on that summer, I was at a party dancing, and after 10 minutes on the dance floor, I had to sit down. I was in so much pain! My feet felt like they were on fire, from the bottom of my feet, to the back of my heel. The pain increased as I tried to walk.

That following Monday, I made an appointment with my doctor who suggested that I see an orthopedic specialist. The specialist explained that because of my stroke, I had a severe limb deformity on my right side. I was walking on the balls of my feet.

Normally, when we walk, it's supposed to be in a heel-to-toe motion, but because the limbs and muscles in my leg and foot were damaged, walking in that heel-toe-motion was impossible. He also explained that there were surgical options but because I was young and still growing, I had to wait until 14-15. In the meantime, there were exercises and orthopedic braces I could try to ease the pain.

The next few months I had a packed schedule. Between school and physical therapy at least three times a week, speaking engagements were on hold indefinitely.

After a few months of physical therapy, my therapist announced at the end of my session one day that he was transferring to Miami Children's Hospital. A colleague knew of an orthopedic foot surgeon who specialized in limb lengthening for children. My therapist said he would talk to his colleague and could get me an appointment to see this surgeon.

A few weeks later, I met Dr. Christopher Iobst. After an exam, he revealed that the tendons and muscles in my right leg were extremely tight and there was one more option he wanted to try before performing surgery. Botox injections! The goal of these injections was to get the muscles in my leg to relax and hopefully allow my foot to be flat on the ground when I walked.

Dr. Iobst referred us to a pediatric neurologist, Dr. Oscar Papazian. My first visit to his office was a humbling experience. In the waiting room were so many children with disabilities that were in way worse conditions than me. I remember feeling somewhat guilty because I was able to walk, talk, and do all these amazing things, while some of the kids in the waiting room would never be able to walk or talk.

After a series of injections, the muscles relaxed and I was finally able to walk somewhat normally. The pain was almost non-existent, I could function. I was happy. I was back to doing speaking engagements again. I had even signed up to be on the Speech and Debate team and been entered in a competition with a few other students from the school.

During my follow-up with Dr. Iobst a few weeks later, he explained that while the injections fixed one problem, they didn't fix the limb lengthening discrepancy. He wanted to address this issue while I was young, so that I didn't encounter hip, back, and knee problems later on in life. So, the summer before eighth grade, I had surgery on my right foot. Eight weeks of recovery and physical therapy was not a bad start to my last year of junior school.

Around that time, we began high school tours. My classmates were looking at a lot of the high schools that were far from where I lived and more expensive, so we had to look at something closer. One day after school, my grandmother called me into her bedroom and said, "You will be attending Archbishop Curley Notre Dame next year,"

"Okay," I said, with no enthusiasm.

"Why did you say it like that?" she asked. "Curley is a good school. That is where your Uncle Todd went."

"Nana, it's just school." I said before turning around and walking away.

None of my friends were attending school at Curley and I really did not feel like making new ones. Something else happened toward the end of eight grade; I had begun to pull away from public speaking. Several of my classmates and I had been selected to participate in an Academic bowl. By the end of that event, I looked over at my grandmother and said, "I don't want to do this anymore, I am done."

Up to this point, I had been an in-demand motivational speaker for 11 years. The gift that had exposed me to so much and introduced me to so many people, I no longer enjoyed.

CHAPTER 4

A lot of people believe that high school is supposed to represent the best years of your life. While that may be true for some, high school for me was a place where I got into a lot of disagreements with my family and learned painful lessons and probably should have been taking schoolwork, tests, and exams more seriously, at least in the beginning.

High school was where I showed my parents that I did not give a shit. My only goal was to finish and move out on my own. Full disclosure, my grades for those first few years weren't the best, particularly in English. Funny, considering that writing is now a big part of my life. The books that we were reading for class did not interest me at all! So, when it came time for testing, I put in the least amount of effort which translated to average grades.

Well, that was unacceptable for my family, particularly my grandmother Marie. So, we had to have a little chat. Here's the thing, we had been having these "chats" about my grades for quite some time and I would always end the conversation with that promise, "I will do better next time," And the next exam would come back with a bad grade.

It wasn't that I was a bad student, I just had no interest in school. After we left a parent-teacher conference one day, my grandmother and I were driving home discussing what she and my English teacher discussed. Things got heated between us.

"You have an exam coming up, and you need to pass it," she said as she came to a stop at a red light.

"Well, I am not going to study for it, " I said. "I really don't care about school anymore."

"If you keep this attitude up, you will fail and you will have to repeat the class over," she said as the light turned green.

"We still have one more quarter left, so I don't see why you are making this such a big deal," I said.

"It's a big deal because I am paying a lot of money for you to attend school here, " she said.

"It's always about the money, isn't it?" I said. "Tell you what, why don't you just stop paying for me to go to school?" Now, I know that sounded really ungrateful, but the truth is I was over this conversation. But her response shocked the hell out of me.

"YOU KNOW WHAT?!? She yelled, "IF THAT'S WHAT YOU WANT ME TO DO, WE WILL GO HOME, YOU CAN PACK ALL OF YOUR STUFF AND I WILL SEND YOU TO YOUR MOM, AND I WILL HAVE NOTHING ELSE TO DO WITH YOU!"

I didn't want to admit it, but seeing her upset made me upset. I understood why, she was my grandmother and she invested in my success, but at that moment, I did not care! I was mad because of her constant nagging over my academic performance.

I sat in complete silence as the hot tears fell down my face on our way home. She went on and on about me needing to tighten up because colleges started looking at grades during junior year. I felt like we would never reach the house. I desperately wanted this car ride to be over.

She then told me how my dad at 16 did not like school and what had become of his life because of the choices he had made. Was she actually implying that I was going to end up like that?

My dad was a hustler, selling dope when I was a baby. The streets were a means to end for him because he had a goal. He wanted to get into Real Estate. The money was a tool to help achieve this goal faster. Unfortunately, he got caught and sent to prison. Now he had to make his money the hard way in construction.

What's funny is, once my dad got out of prison, he never went back. No matter what he did in the streets, he made sure no harm ever came to me. I had no desire to follow that path. So why was my grandmother even thinking that about me?

We had finally reached home. She parked the car in the driveway and sat in silence for a while.

"What happened to you?" she asked.

"I have gotten older, I am not a kid anymore." I said. "Why are you making such a big deal out of this?"

"I am just trying to give you some guidance," she said.

"Well, your guidance is not helping me at all right now." I unbuckled my seat belt and stormed inside the house.

As I entered my bedroom, I threw my bookbag on the floor and crawled into bed. For a few moments, I laid perfectly still with my eyes closed, trying to give my heart rate a moment to decelerate. I opened my eyes a few seconds later and looked around my room at all of the awards and trophies that I won for speaking engagements through the years and became even more enraged.

"Why me God?" I asked. "Why did you have to give me the Gift of Gab?"

For the next few months, I continued with this below average academic performance. It definitely caused a lot of disagreements between my grandparents and I. The one person who didn't argue about it was my dad.

"Buddy, just like the system is not designed for everyone to be rich, the system is not designed for everyone to bring home straight A's," he said as we were riding in the car one day along South Beach. My dad was teaching me a valuable lesson about success.

"But some kids do bring home straight A's," I said.

"Those kids are exceptions to the rule," he said. "I am not saying you slack off and be lazy. I am not saying good grades are not important, and I am not saying you can't be at the top of your class. I am saying, do not put all this unnecessary pressure on yourself."

This conversation with my dad put my mind at ease. It gave me a different outlook on how I would approach the remainder of my junior year, with positivity and optimism.

CHAPTER 5

The beginning of my senior year was crazy! By the end of the first quarter, I had achieved Principal's Honors and straight a's in five of my six classes. I loved this new energy that I had found for my schoolwork. Shortly before Thanksgiving break, my dad suffered a near fatal stroke. All the years of neglecting his high blood pressure had caught up to him.

It was a Sunday morning. My dad and his friend Ronnie were getting ready to go fishing on Tamiami Trail, one their fishing spots. I was supposed to go to church that morning, but for some reason, I decided to stay home. As my dad was waiting for Ronnie to get ready, we were sitting in the living room watching the morning news. I noticed he kept turning the volume up.

"What are you doing?" I asked.

"I can't hear it," he said.

A few moments later, he said, "My head feels really tight," For years, my dad had really bad headaches, but never nothing like this. Within seconds, he started sweating like he had just got out of the shower and forgot to dry off. His t-shirt was drenched.

He jumped up from the couch and rushed into his bedroom to dry off and change his shirt. He rushed back into the front room and begged my grandfather to call 911. By the time he sat down in a chair in the front room, his entire left side went dead!

For me, watching my dad who was completely fine the day before suddenly fade away in front of me was shocking and scary at the same time.

Shortly after arriving at the hospital, the doctor informed us that my dad had suffered a right-side hemorrhagic stroke. The doctor explained that a teaspoon of blood had gotten on his brain and, had he been out on the water, he would not have survived.

Dad stayed in the hospital for one month and had to learn how to walk again. While he was in the hospital, it was as if all the new-found energy I had gotten at the start of the school year decreased. My dad was someone I saw every single day, and we laughed and talked about everything. Now suddenly not having that and not knowing what the outcome would be had my emotions all over the place.

The same prayer warriors that prayed for me must have prayed for him because one month later, Dad came home in time for Christmas.

Around that time, many of my classmates were busy with SAT/ACT Testing and sending applications to different colleges. Although my grades senior year were exceptional, I wasn't the student who had his top five colleges picked out.

Part of me didn't even know if I wanted to go to college. If I did decide to go, I knew I wanted to stay local, and I did not want to study Mass Communications, Broadcast Production, or Radio. My grandmother however, was not hearing that.

One day after school, she tells me that she got the number and address to a technical school in Doral for, you guessed it, Broadcast Production.

"Nana, I already told you, I am not interested in that," I said.

"Well, what are you interested in?" she asked.

"I have no idea, but I know it's not this," I responded.

"Well, just go check it out. You might meet someone there who might be doing something else," she said.

Later on, that evening we arrived at the school. The director and representatives are talking with all the prospective students about the different programs available and what students could expect. As they are talking, I am looking around the room trying to decide whether to walk out the front door as one of the representatives approaches me and my grandmother.

After introducing himself, he looks over at me and asks what program I am interested in.

"I'm not sure, I will come back when and if I make up MY mind!" I responded sharply, giving my grandmother a look.

The representative chuckled lightly. I think he could tell by the look on my face that I was not interested. Rather than carry on the conversation, he politely thanked us for coming and moved on to the next student.

"Can we go now?" I asked my grandmother.

A few weeks later, while on my way to lunch, my English teacher and college advisor, Mrs. Panareli, stopped me in the hallway and asked me what my intentions as far as college was concerned.

"You're one of a handful of students that hasn't come by my office to talk to me. What's going on?" she asked.

"The thing is, I am not sure if I want to go," I responded.

"Come by the office after school and we will talk about it," she said.

So, I found myself inside her office talking about some of the frustration I had been having as far as career and college. She suggested Saint Thomas University.

"It's a small school, it's local, and quite a few students have graduated from here and gone there and done really well. The deadline to apply is coming up so you need to make a decision soon," she said.

I remembered that name because a few months before we had one of the professors from Saint Thomas, Dr Conley came out and talked to our class.

A few days later, my grandmother went out to the university and picked up an application and brochure. When I sat down to fill everything out, she insisted that I select Mass Communications.

"You're just not going to let this go, are you?" I sighed, rolling my eyes.

"Well, what are you going to put down?" she asked.

"Undeclared," I snorted as I checked the box and put the application in the envelope. Now the waiting game began.

By now it's the middle of march, my senior year is quickly winding down. Most of my classmates were already receiving acceptance letters from their colleges of choice.

One day after school, I came home and there was a letter from Saint Thomas University Office of Admissions.

"Oh God," my grandmother said anxiously.

I quickly opened the letter and read the opening lines of the first paragraph, then looked up at my grandparents.

"Well, what does it say?" They asked.

"I got in," I grinned. And to my surprise, the university also wanted to offer me a scholarship.

My grandparents, including my great-grandmother Mattie, quickly pulled me in for a hug and congratulated me. Within seconds my grandmother was calling all of her friends to tell them the good news.

I called my great-grandmother Catherine and told her that I had been accepted.

"That's great baby," she enthused. Baby is her nickname for me. Even to this day, she will tell anybody, "I raised him from a baby, and it does matter if he lives to be a 100, he will still be my baby."

My mother, Tonya, was the next person I called. "I know that's right!" she yelled. "Do you know what you are going to study?"

"Not yet," I said.

Even with all the celebrations that happened those last few weeks of senior year, I still had a big decision to make about this next chapter in my life.

CHAPTER 6

I started college in the fall of 2009. After months of disagreements with my family, I finally declared a major. I had enrolled in the Bachelors of Communication Arts program. But I was still directionless. I didn't have a plan for the next four years of my life. So, I asked God for guidance, clarity, and purpose. Finally, a professor pulled me aside after class one day and we started a conversation that changed my entire outlook.

Dr. Philip Shepardson was my speech professor during my first semester at St. Thomas University. One of our assignments was to recite a poem. As a motivational speaker growing up, reciting poems was something that came natural. However, it had been quite a few years since I had spoken in front of a crowd.

As it turns out, Dr. Shepardson was impressed with my delivery. So, after class that day, he pulled me aside and said, "Your delivery was excellent, but I sense that something is troubling you."

"Honestly Dr. Shepardson, I am not happy because I am not sure what I am supposed to be doing. I am not sure what I want to do after college." I said, taking a seat on a bench next to him.

"You just started, you have four years to think about that," he said.

We spoke about all of my accomplishments, college majors, career possibilities, and opportunities in the field of communications. Dr. Shepardson suggested I take a TV Production course.

"This is where you learn how to produce your own TV Show," he said. "You will also learn how to edit footage, and other technical aspects of television production."

It sounded like a cool class. I let our conversation marinate in the back of my mind for the rest of that first semester.

It's amazing when you ask for guidance and clarity, how it can reveal itself. It can come in the form of a kind stranger, or a conversation. Often times, it comes when you least expect it.

Fast forward to my junior year. I had flown through most of the introductory courses with flying colors. I was well into taking the classes for my major. I took Dr. Shepardson's advice and signed up for the Introduction to Television Production course. In that course we learned the basics of video editing, and how to produce news segments. Although this course taught me the fundamentals, I still did not feel fulfilled. I had already decided that Broadcast Journalism was not the career path. I still needed guidance and clarity.

It just so happened that, in the class, I reconnected with someone I knew from high school. He, and a few of his friends were a couple semesters ahead of me, and they wanted to do film production. Our professor informed us that she would be teaching the advanced course and that we would have complete creative freedom to produce whatever we wanted. My friend encouraged me to take the Advanced TV Production class with him and his friends the next semester.

"I'm in," I said.

So, that following semester I was registered for Advanced TV Production. There were 10 of us in the class. Our first assignment was to outline a concept for a show and have it ready to discuss in class the following week.

That following week, I walked in class and my mind was blank. *Was I really about to fail this class a week into the semester?* As we sat around discussing our ideas, one of my classmates, Chris, said he wanted to produce a TV series focused on two of our classmates who were soccer players. As I listened, I came up with a concept: A show-within a show. I would follow him and his crew around and film behind the scenes footage.

A few weeks later, we began production on a series called *A University Horror Story.* The concept wa: two friends uncover a mystery that happened on campus a few years prior. Watching my classmates produce this series was honestly a master class in film production. Their work ethic was fast paced but organized. I was truly having a blast for the first time in a while. I wanted to do more of this.

By the end of the end of semester, I had finally found something that I could see myself doing and enjoying.

CHAPTER 7

In the Fall of 2012, my mom and I are on our way home from dinner. That's our thing, random dinner dates to catch up. As we were driving along the expressway, I looked up at a billboard and saw that the Powerball jackpot was $580 million. We talked about all of the things we would do if we caught the jackpot because, who doesn't? Suddenly, I blurted out, "I would start my own production company,"

"Ooooh, I like that!" Mom responded. "Put a business plan together."

My mother is an entrepreneur. She has been a licensed cosmetologist for 32 years and has a skill for turning small ideas into big money. So, for her to hear me say that I wanted to start my own business was like music to her ears. It was a bold idea that hit me out of nowhere.

A few days later after class, I was inside a cafe inside St. Thomas University's school of Law. This cafe was a hidden gem that I discovered thanks to one of my classmates showing up to class one morning with cafe con leche and Cuban toast. If you are from Miami, you know that that is considered a delicacy by many and is one of my favorite breakfast meals. I had been coming to this cafe for a few months and had made friends with one of the owners, Rudy, and his family. On this particular day, I walked in and Rudy introduced me to his brother, Marc. We shook hands and I ordered lunch.

As I sat down at the table, Marc came up to me and asked, "Hey brother, I couldn't help but notice your hand, how did that happen?" Most people would be embarrassed or shut down at the idea of talking about their disability. But I wasn't. That question began a conversation that ended 3 hours later.

In those three hours, it was as if I had known this dude my whole life. We talked about everything, including the crossroads we were at in our lives. Marc shared that he had several jobs in corporate America and was now deciding on starting his own business or attending law school.

Marc also shared with me that he too had a disability that caused him a lot of physical pain over the years. The fact that we had so much in common made me feel a lot better about myself. It meant I still had a lot of learning and growing to do, and that was okay.

The Jacir brothers, like a lot of other people I have met over the years, are examples of people who you have an instant connection with. You know that they are in your life for the long haul.

A few nights later, my mom called. We were laughing about the fact that it was not us who had won the $580 Million Powerball Jackpot. She then started telling me about an idea she had for a reality TV show. After hearing her pitch and the backstory, I was intrigued because this idea was something that was not being done on television. I was excited for my mom because I could hear the excitement and the passion in her voice. One thing about my mom, she is driven and when she puts her mind to something, she is all in!

For the next few weeks, I watched my mom go from cosmetologist to TV Producer. She was getting EVERYONE involved. She even had a Social Media page for the show and was being featured in local magazines. Watching my mom go from idea to execution was inspiring.

In May of 2013, I graduated with my bachelor's degree in Communication Arts from St. Thomas University. Many of my classmates had gotten job offers, some were even applying to graduate programs to begin their masters degrees. I, on the other hand, needed a break from school to see what other opportunities were out there. But my grandparents weren't having it.

"Don't take too much time off, because if you stop, you won't want to go back." I heard these words from everybody. Family members, family friends, professors. Truth be told, I didn't want to jump back into a Master's program because I still felt incomplete, like I did not do enough in college because I was so focused on making good grades.

You would think with all the people I had met over the years through public speaking that finding a job would be easy, but that wasn't the case. You see, one of the downsides of just focusing on school was that I got comfortable. When you get too comfortable, you stop learning, you stop growing, you stop evolving.

LESSON 1: DO NOT GET COMFORTABLE

If you could go back and have a conversation with your younger self, what would you say? I would say, DO NOT GET COMFORTABLE! We live in a time where it is harder for people to get ahead and stay ahead. Just having a fancy degree and good grades is not enough. In order to get ahead and stay ahead, you will have to do things that make you uncomfortable.

When I started college, I got government assistance. That stream of income, along with the support of my family, allowed me to focus on school and not have to worry about the bills. After college, I managed to save up a decent amount of money and that check continued to come in, so I really was not in a big rush to look for a job after graduation. I was comfortable.

Confession number two, I am a homebody. If I have to choose between going out on a Friday or Saturday night or staying home in my pajamas watching reruns of my favorite shows, guess which one I am choosing?

Being an introvert does not mean you are lazy! It just means that is how you recharge. Also, the choice I made to continue to receive my disability benefits does not make a bad person. Now, you might be reading this and thinking, *"You are out of your mind! Go get a job! Any job!* The truth is, I had a huge problem with that logic. I was already very conflicted, and I did not want to feel like I was settling for less just because that opening was available. I knew I could do better for myself, I just had to find the right opportunity.

Maybe you are where I was, you're directionless, and you have no idea what your next step is. Maybe you have a bold idea, but you don't know how to get started. You don't have it all figured out and you feel like a failure because you are not moving as fast as everyone else and that makes you uncomfortable.

First, take a breath! You don't have to have all of the answers right now, but you do have to take that first step, no matter how uncomfortable it might be. So you might be wondering how do you do that?

First, **identify** where you want to go. For me, this was the hard part because I had no direction. It also didn't help that after graduation, I was exposed to so many possibilities and paths, and had several people in my ear telling me go down this path, or don't go down that route. Oftentimes, it is hard to hear your own voice and follow your heart when you are surrounded by the opinions of others.

My advice is write down all the things you want to do, including your passions and your skills, and see which one resonates with you the most. Then go out and find any opportunity to showcase your skills and your passions.

Let's say you have identified that you want to be a speaker, but you are terrified of speaking on stages. Pick up your smartphone, record that message, and upload it to social media. Congrats, you took the first step. Now continue to do that.

We live in a world where you do not have to settle for less. But that does not mean be lazy! Do the uncomfortable thing that terrifies you, follow your heart, put in the work, and trust me, something will pay off.

CHAPTER 8

A few months into my post-graduation vacation, I got a call from an old classmate of mine from St. Thomas University. Her name was Rayshawn Coleman. We had taken a religious studies class together during undergrad and instantly hit it off. However, she had transferred from St Thomas during my junior year and we lost touch. A few months before I finished undergrad, we reconnected and had been having some deeply enlightening and hilarious conversations. So, she calls me up and says, "Hey bro, you gotta get into this TV show called "Revenge." It's a bit soap opera-ish, but I think you will like it,"

I grew up watching soap operas. My grandmother watches them religiously and still does to this day. When I was in undergrad, I would watch a few of them after finishing assignments or taking a break from studying and I had seen the advertisements for Revenge but, I really wasn't into much TV after graduation. So, I told Rayshawn I would check it out and let her know what I thought of it.

So, a few nights later, I decided to check out the pilot episode of "Revenge" on Netflix and I was hooked! By the end of the night, I had binge-watched half the first season.

"Revenge" became our Sunday ritual. Every Sunday, we would Skype and watch the show. In between commercial breaks, we would laugh and recite our favorite lines of dialogue which would later on become the butt of a lot of inside jokes. It gave us another way to connect and I loved it. But something else happened during this experience. I found myself being intrigued by the thought of writing a TV show. *What if I could take what I learned in college and apply it to this? What if?*

LESSON 2: BUILD YOUR OWN DAMNED TABLE

So, you graduate college, and don't have a job lined up. But you have an idea for a small business or a concept for a TV show. Do not be afraid to create your own opportunities.

Shortly before the second season of "Revenge" began, I started writing. At the time, I had no idea about how to format a screenplay, I had no idea that there was software that could make the challenge of formatting easier. All I knew was, I enjoyed writing. So, I came up with a concept for a crime-mystery. I called up a few friends and we would have these brainstorming sessions. We went through several rounds of drafts, and nothing seemed to excite me so I stopped. But every Sunday as I kept watching "Revenge" I was inspired to keep working on my story.

One night while talking on the phone with Rayshawn, I shared the screenplay with her. After reading it, she said, "This needs a major overhaul," So we started re-working the plot and further developing the characters. While Rayshawn and I were having these writing sessions, she revealed to me that she loves film and would love to be a filmmaker, but she took a different path, one that she wasn't really enjoying.

Having a little experience in that department, I shared with her my emotional exhaustion with college and being unfulfilled. I then shared with her that I wanted to start my own production company.

"Maaaan, that's dope!" she said.

"What if the two of us teamed up and built our production company?" *What if?*

No one I knew had a goal like that, especially fresh out of college. I started doing my research on the industry, and several things I read all highlighted that if you wanted to make it in entertainment you had to relocate to Los Angeles. I didn't want to do that, at least not yet. After all, I was born and raised in the magic city of Miami. And also, I recalled, a lot of hit movies were filmed in Miami. Bad Boys, 2 Fast 2 Furious, All About the Benjamins. But over the years, the film industry in Florida was not getting enough tax breaks and incentives. So, actors and producers were moving to other states like Atlanta and California.

What if I use my own money? I thought. Armed with this information, I wanted to build my production company right here in Miami.

I shared this idea with my mom during one of our dinner dates. She shared with me that a major TV network had offered her a deal for her reality show, but she felt that the network had low balled her. So, instead of scrapping it, she was going to hold off on pitching it to another work, because she felt that there were better offers out there.

To be honest, I was bummed about the idea falling through. I wanted it to work out because that would have been a foot-in-the-door towards getting a job in the entertainment industry. But it just was not our season. God apparently had something better planned for me. As my mom likes to say, "Nothing will happen before divine order."

That's when I knew I wanted to build my own table.

CHAPTER 9

In the spring of 2014, I still was soul searching for answers. I was pondering the idea of a master's program, but was unsure what track to go down. A master's degree in communications seemed like I was putting all my eggs in one basket. I was stuck... again!

I then called my best friend from college, Natasha and she said that she was back in school at St Thomas pursuing the master's in management. Natasha and I had met in undergrad and immediately clicked. We motivated each other. Many nights, we would have to talk each other through a discussion post or a research paper.

I was surprised that Natasha was back in school so soon. She had just started working for Power96 radio station in the promotions department.

"Isn't management like a lot of math?" I asked. Math was not my best subject. Plus, I had a few classmates who were business majors in undergrad and most of their classes involved accounting, economics, statistics and calculus.

"Not necessarily boo," she said. "This program only has one finance course. Most of it is a lot of writing."

Natasha also told me that several of our classmates from the communications program were pursuing a master's in management.

"You should check it out," she said. "I promise it's not that bad."

I checked out the curriculum. It seemed okay, but I still wasn't sure. Then, I asked myself an important question. *Does this align with your goals?* This vision of my production company was still brewing in my mind. Then I thought, *What if you are seated across from some studio executives pitching a script? Wouldn't it be beneficial to talk on their level?*

A few days later, my great-grandmother Mattie and I are at the kitchen table, talking. Her favorite cooking show, *The Pioneer Lady,* was on in the background. That was our thing. When my grandparents were out running errands, my grandmother Mattie and I would sit and talk for hours about everything as she watched her cooking shows.

"Have you made a decision about your masters yet?" she asked.

"I think I have Grandma," I replied. "I know I want to go back to St. Thomas, but I don't know what program just yet."

"Do you know how much it will cost?" she asked.

"No, but I can check," I said.

"Let me know, I am willing to help pay for it," she said.

I had to mentally process what my great-grandmother had just said to me. She was 92 years old and the fact that she was willing to invest in my education meant the world to me. It also meant I had to make a decision, and fast!

<u>LESSON 3: SAY YES</u>

I probably said no to graduate school at least 20 times before I decided to enroll. My grandmother Marie was an educator who earned her master's degree because during her time, a master's degree meant more money. At this stage in my life, I was tired of school and the thought of another 2 years in school was not something I was looking forward to. But…I had someone willing to help me ease the financial burden. Many of my friends and classmates who were pursuing their degrees were in debt and paying for their degrees on their own. It was stressful for a lot of them which brings me to point: SAY YES TO HELP.

If you have someone in your life that is willing to invest in your future, don't be stupid, say yes! Now, I want to be clear, I understand that not everyone has, or will have, that kind of family support, but if you do, DO NOT TAKE IT FOR GRANTED!

My grandmother Marie told me the story of an ex-co-worker who was PE coach at her school. While he was working, he purchased bonds that he was going to use to pay for his kid's college education. When the time came, the daughter went but the son did not. So, the father took the unused money and purchased a home in another state. A few years after purchasing that house, the son came back to him, and said he wanted to go to college, but it was too late. The father told him that was a one-time offer. The father died a few years later.

Even if you don't use that degree right away, guess what? It's paid for and you don't have to stop or put life on hold to go back to school. When you have someone offering a helping hand, take their damn hand!

CHAPTER 10

By the fall of 2014, I was back in school starting my master's degree. Graduate school is much faster than undergrad. My semesters were 8 weeks long vs a semester in Undergrad is 16 weeks. I learned how to finish assignments a lot quicker which taught me an important lesson in Entrepreneurship.

LESSON 4: PERFECTION IS NOT THE ANSWER

Here is another confession: I have a huge problem with overthinking. My mom often says that smart people procrastinate a lot and I think that is because we as people, overthink. Why do we overthink? It's because of this lie that we continue to tell ourselves that we are not good enough. I don't know when this started for me, but, before becoming a writer, I was not a person who could make decisions and see it through without overthinking the details.

In the beginning, it really affected my writing because I was not confident. I would write a couple of pages and if my writing did not mirror what I was seeing on TV, I would stop. I wanted it to be perfect the first time around. But here is the thing, it is not going to be perfect the first time and you have to be okay with that. It's part of growth.

During one semester of undergrad, I was taking Advanced TV Production. I produced an interview show where I talked to different local leaders in the City of Miami. That was my first YouTube video, my first time conducting an interview, and it was terrible. Search Everyday Miami Episode 1:

1. I am not seated side by side like some conducting an interview
2. My back is to the camera
3. I am reading my questions off a sheet of paper!

I am a speaker, I have been on TV before, what the hell is wrong with me? Now the perfectionist part of me wanted to scrap it, but there was no time. I was on a deadline. Even though those first videos weren't the best, I still managed to win an award for Best Talent that next semester.

Perfection keeps you stuck, it keeps from finishing your projects, it keeps you from accomplishing goals, and you never move to the next level. Finish your projects! Write that script, write that book, launch that product! The world is waiting for you to show up! You got this!

My first class in graduate school was a research methods class. This course prepared you for graduate level writing and research. As a student with a communications background, writing wasn't difficult for me. In fact, it was natural to me. My ONLY assignment that semester was a 25-page research paper! The professor gave us the freedom to write about any topic we wanted.

I didn't have 16 weeks to sit around and overthink. We had to have our topic picked and an informal outline ready the following week. By the end of class that night, I was ready to go home and withdraw from school because it was insane to me!

What the hell was I going to write 25 pages on? I thought. *How is this going to help me land a job, or start a business?*

A few days later, I was sitting at home watching reruns of the soap opera "One Life to Live." I had discovered it late in 2010 when the soap opera, "As The World Turns" was canceled by CBS. This genre was being canceled because it was expensive to produce, and networks were looking for ways to save money. They were being replaced by talk shows.

Suddenly, a light bulb went off. I could write my research paper on this very topic.

Me writing an academic research paper on Daytime Soap Operas. Me writing a paper on anything in the media is weird because I didn't want a thing to do with this industry four and half years ago.

But as I am writing it, a feeling comes over me. A feeling of curiosity. What if this research could be used in my business? What if I could revamp the Soap Opera Genre?

After all, a man can dream, can't he?

As I am conducting my research to begin writing this paper, mostly all of the sources are saying the same thing: The decline of Daytime Soap Operas was because they were no longer profitable for the networks and their advertising partners. The annual cost to produce a soap opera is $40-50 million a year.

Instead of being turned off by how much money was needed, I was motivated to continue looking for ways to get started. Maybe I didn't have the funds to produce a full-length, hour-long soap opera or a full length 20-episode TV show, but...what I did have was vision, determination, and creativity. All I needed to do now was get started and someone to listen.

CHAPTER 11

By the Fall of 2016, I was a semester away from finishing my masters and I found myself in a familiar mindset just like when I finished my bachelor's degree. I did not want to settle for less than I deserved. I know most of you reading this are probably thinking,
"Dude, who do you think you are?"

Here is the problem with settling as I said back in Chapter 7. Once you settle, you stop evolving, you get comfortable, and suddenly all the big ideas and plans you have for yourself go to the graveyard to die.

That semester, I took a class called *Organizational Design & Theory.* Essentially, I learned how an organization was built and structured. The professor, Dr. Lisa Knowles, and I had met each other in passing on campus but this was my first time taking a class. Her energy, and her personality instantly drew me to her. We instantly had a connection, similar to that of Dr. Shepardson and I. Her style of teaching was engaging and open.

Our final assignment was to develop an organizational plan for the company we currently worked for, or a business we would like to start one day. Immediately, my production company idea came to mind. So, I got work crafting the plan. A few weeks later, we got our grades back, and at the top of my paper was a hand-written message that read: *I want to see you put this together.*

I have to admit, reading that message, I was surprised. It is hard to get the people close to you to listen to your ideas or read them. But then there are people like Dr Knowles who take an interest in you and what you have to offer. After class was over, I caught up with Dr. Knowles and we chatted about my assignment.

"Ray, I loved your organizational plan. How long have you had this idea?" she asked.

"About 4 years," I responded.

We talked about how the idea of my production company was created and why I wanted to start one. Dr. Knowles shared that she was on the Broward Workforce Development Board. The film industry in South Florida was often a topic of conversation at some of their meetings.

"You could be just what the film industry needs Ray. Continue working on your plan and developing your work. I am rooting for you."

I left class with a new-found sense of motivation. I was going to continue to work on my business. What if Dr Knowles was right, and I was someone the film industry needed in South Florida?

LESSON 5: FIND YOURSELF A MENTOR

This might sound cliche but GET YOURSELF A MENTOR! When I first began public speaking, the closest thing I had to a mentor was Delrish Moss. This entire process was new to me. I was six years old. I did not know anything about marketing, branding, or charging for a speech. But watching Delrish, I learned a lot from him about speaking and being an effective communicator.

Now, at this stage in my journey, my mentors are Dr Knowles and Shaun Grant. I met Shaun Grant on Instagram. I checked out his page and discovered he was an actor, writer, and a coach. I knew he was
someone I wanted to learn from. I wanted to pick his brain on his process and how he got started.

Here is another piece of advice on Mentorship. Make sure that the person you choose to be your mentor can actually help you achieve your goals. For example, let's say your goal is to write a book. Your mentor should definitely be someone who has written a book before.

Throughout my journey as a public speaker, I have shaken hands, taken pictures and had dinner with hundreds of people all over the City of Miami. I am talking about local TV and radio personalities, local politicians, community leaders, athletes, actors, CEO's, the list goes on. I said that, not to brag, but to instill in you that **EVERYONE YOU COME ACROSS IS NOT A MENTOR!**

For example, if you want to be a surgeon, would you trust an accountant to guide you through a 7-hour surgery? Probably not. I have seen people choose a mentor based on their social media following. Then, when it comes time to look at their business plan or strategies, that "mentor" has absolutely no idea what the hell you are talking about, because they have someone else doing that task for them.

When selecting a mentor, do not be afraid to check their credentials. Ask them who have they helped? What have they done? This is a person you will be spending a lot of time with when you are starting
your journey. Choose wisely!

CHAPTER 12

It's May 13, 2017, Graduation Day again. But this time, the feeling is different.

Don't get me wrong, I am excited to be walking across the stage, but my mind is on something else: My Grandmother Mattie's health is declining which makes me sad. As I mentioned earlier, she invested in my education, and I wanted her to see this moment.

After the ceremony, my mom and grandparents wanted to take me to dinner to celebrate. But I told them there was something I needed to do first.

I went home and my grandmother Mattie was in her bedroom sleeping. She had Stage four arthritis. The pain I watched her go through, I would not wish on my worst enemy.

"Grandma, are you awake?" I whispered.

She slowly opens her eyes and she looks at me dressed in my cap and gown and through the pain and the sleep, she smiles.

"You look so good, and I am so proud of you," she said.

"Thank you, Grandma. I couldn't have done it with you. I love you," I kissed her forehead.

Five days later on May 18, 2017, my grandmother passed away. I The day had started with a trip to the car dealership to get my car serviced. On the way, my grandmother Marie called me and my dad from the hospital.

"Your grandmother wants to see you. Get here now!" she said.

We had put my great-grandmother Mattie in the hospital two days prior. She said she wasn't feeling well and she wanted to go to the hospital. In the days and weeks leading up to the 18th, she had expressed how tired she was and that she was ready to go. But clearly, she had unfinished business.

When my dad and I arrived at the hospital about 30 minutes later, my great-grandmother was resting comfortably. We didn't have to say anything when we walked into her hospital room. It was as if she knew we were there. She opened her eyes and I could see this sadness in them like she didn't want my dad or me to see her like that.

I leaned close to her, kissed her forehead, and told her how much I loved her.

We went home and I needed to distract myself. So, I called my best friend Rayshawn and we started talking about our scripts. Writing was our escape from all the things going on in our lives.

By 11 p.m., Rayshawn and I were deep into our writing. My dad came into the sunroom and told me the hospital called. My great-grandmother's blood pressure was dropping and they needed us there at the hospital.

Thirty minutes later, my dad called and he was crying.

"Grandma is gone!" he cried.

Everything in my head went silent. I ended the call with Rayshawn and went to my great-grandmother's room and cried.

From the day I moved with my dad and my grandparents George and Marie in sixth grade until now, my great-grandmother Mattie was always there. Every day I would come home from school, she would be sitting at the dinner table. The moment I walked in, she would smile and ask me about my day.

I recall a conversation we had a few years ago. My grandfather George had made an absurd remark at breakfast one morning. It is a part of his charm. While my grandparents were out running errands, my grandmother Mattie and I were talking about it, and I related the remark to a joke that Wanda Sykes had made in one of her stand-ups. My great-grandmother Mattie burst out laughing. She thought it was the funniest thing ever.

Those are the memories I keep close to my heart.

CHAPTER 13

Early in 2018, I was invited to attend my friend Frederica Burden's book signing. I first met Frederica while interning at the City of Miami Police Department. She had recently retired and wrote her first book, a thriller, called "Miami Beat."

"You should go, you might run into someone you know." My grandmother Marie said.

She wanted me to network, still holding onto hope that six years later I would change my mind about breaking into TV and Media. Don't get me wrong, I did want to break into TV, just not broadcasting.

The thought of attending this event however, makes me a little annoyed. I started scratching my head. My grandmother already knows the means, *I do not want to go.* It's not that I don't want to support my friend because I do. It's the idea of running into someone I know and having that exhausting small talk.

"Hey, what have you been to lately? What are you doing with yourself now?"

As if you owe this person a play-by-play of your life. It's the kind of conversation that makes me question whether or not I want to attend this signing, or whether or not I want to stay home and write.

My grandmother shook her head and let out this long sigh. I know what she is thinking. She's thinking I am letting my degrees and my skills just waste away. I know that my parents, grandparents, and friends held me in high regard because of what happened to me and my abilities.

But I was adopting a new identity for myself, and it was already making people uncomfortable.

Regardless, I told Frederica I would show up for her, and I was going to keep that promise.

So, the day of Frederica's signing arrives. I show up, hug her, and talk to a few people I know from the PD and the event gets underway. As I am listening to Frederica read from her book, something clicks off in my brain.

This is really cool, I think. Seeing a friend of mine launch her brand and become an author was inspiring. That meant that success as a writer was possible.

Later that evening, I started reading Frederica's book and I was hooked! The characters, the storyline, everything, was amazing.

I get a lot of inspiration for story ideas from reading. When I graduated with my bachelor's degree and took that post-graduation vacation, not only did I get hooked on TV shows, I also started reading again. I picked up one of James Patterson's books while shopping at Costco one day. I loved his edge-of-your-seat, fast-paced style of storytelling.

My grandmother Marie instilled in me the importance of reading because that's our thing. Her favorite author is Danielle Steel, so every time we read a new book, we will share details with each other.

Now I am reading Frederica's book, I am inspired to write. I had this same feeling as I did when I started watching "Revenge." By the end of the night, something else had clicked off in my brain.

I wanted to become an author. I already knew what to do. *Start Writing.*

<u>LESSON 6: START</u>

I read a Social Media post a while back that said, "Think about all the box office hits we will never see. Think about all the New York Times, best-selling books we will never read because the writer gave up."

I will take it a step further and say that writer never got started.

Let's face it, putting your work or ideas out there is scary! But in order for your work or ideas to become anything, you have to start! The hardest part of getting in shape is telling yourself to get up off the couch and go to the gym. Once you start, you develop a routine.

I bet that at some point in your life, you had an idea that you would like to execute.

But somehow, you never start. Something always stops you from writing the first paragraph of that book, writing the opening scene for that screenplay, or you convince yourself that you can't quit your job to start that business.

What's even more interesting is that often we are jealous or envious of those that do. We think there is some secret to their fast success. Or we say, "they got lucky,"

My grandfather loves to pride himself on how hard he had to work to build the life he did. My grandparents grew up in a time where entrepreneurship was a fairytale. They obtained their success through working for someone else. So, when my grandfather sees someone else achieve success faster than he did, there is always a hint of envy in his voice along with fear.

"Do you know how long that is going to take?

"What if it fails?

My question to these questions is: how do I know if something will or won't work if I don't try?"

Fear is a powerful weapon and if you allow it to consume your thoughts, your drive, and your ambition, you will not achieve success.

There are so many tools and opportunities out there in today's world that makes achieving success easier.

I believe anyone can create the life they want. All you have to do is make a decision, and start!

CHAPTER 14

I have a pretty simple morning routine. I wake up, wash my face, brush my teeth, make coffee, watch a bit of the local news, and read a few chapters of a book while sipping coffee. It gets my creative juices flowing for the day.

One morning, I was in the sunroom. The sunroom used to be our back porch until my grandfather and grandmother decided a few years ago to close it in and make it another room. It's where I get most of my reading and writing done. My dad came in and said, "You wanna ride with me?"

"Sure," I said, finishing up the chapter and ran to get dressed. Any opportunity I have to go off with my dad, I take. I love car rides with him because we always end up laughing or talking about anything and everything.

"Where are we going?" I asked as we got in the car a few minutes later.

"Dade County Building Department," he said.

It didn't sound fun but what the hell, it was a chance to get out from behind my computer screen.

We arrive at the building department about 30 minutes later, and the minute we enter, I notice this place is buzzing. Every window has a line of at least 7 people in it. My dad just shakes his head and signs us in. We walk to a small waiting area which is packed and wait for our number to be called. As I watch these people at the window, something clicks off in my brain.

It's 10 am on a Tuesday, and this place is crawling with people. They all have paperwork in their hands. What is going on?

"What were all those people doing back there?" I asked my dad about 45 minutes later when we got back into the car.

He explained to me that most of those people work on behalf of the contractor because the contractor himself cannot leave the job site to process that paperwork.

"That's a real job?" I asked.

"Oh yes, and a necessary one too. No major building project can start without a permit," he said.

"So, what degree or skills do you have to get that job?" I asked, intrigued.

"No degree necessarily. You just have to have an understanding of the process. I'll show you."

"How much do they get paid?" I asked.

"Some of those guys get $200-300 dollars per project." My dad responded.

Immediately, I started doing some quick math in my head because I saw an opportunity.

LESSON 7: LEARN A NEW SKILL

Maybe you are a recent college graduate, maybe you have worked a job for at least two to three years, and you are looking to move to the next level in your career. Maybe you are testing the waters of entrepreneurship for the first time, and you are trying to figure out how to make it work. Regardless of where you are in your professional life right now, the last thing you want to hear is Learn a New Skill. But in reality, it might be just what you need to do to get to the next level.

When I graduated with my Masters in 2017, I had a better idea of the path I wanted to go down, just not how I was going to make it work. How was I going to bring this vision to life? I had gone on a few job interviews, but they were all for these customer service jobs or sales positions, like the young men you see selling cable packages in Walmart. Although those jobs would have provided me with an income, they weren't going to help me achieve my goals as a writer.

This might sound like an over-inflated sense of self-worth, but I have said before, and I will say it again. I don't believe in settling for less than I deserve, especially when you have a wide range of skills that you can use to make money.

So, when my dad introduced me to permit running as a side hustle, I jumped at it because it helped learn a new skill, provided me with extra income, as well as gave me freedom and flexibility to work on other projects.

If you are unhappy with your job or where you are in your life, learn a new skill. Be open minded to learning new things and learning them quickly. The faster you can learn something, the faster you can be on a new path towards a better life.

CHAPTER 15

September 2018, I receive a phone call from Sharon Hallback. We were in a Church Bowling League together and she instantly took a liking to me. She gave herself the title of my surrogate mom and I greatly accepted her into my life as a part of my family. To me, she is Momma Hallback.

Our typical conversation starts off with a bit of Spanish gibberish. She laughs hysterically, I laugh, and our conversation continues about our love of jazz music, or what tv shows we may be watching.

Momma Hallback worked in Human Resources for several years at a variety of companies across South Florida. She knew my educational background, and I shared that I was directionless in what my next steps were. So, she would always call to check in and offer some form of encouragement.

Except, this particular phone call wasn't about career advice.

"Hey son, what are you doing on October 10, at 10 a.m.?" she asked.

"Hey Momma, nothing at the moment, what's up?" I replied

"I was wondering if you would like to speak at a Career Workshop I am hosting in a few weeks," she asked.

I pause for at least a few seconds because there is no way she just asked me to speak at an event. Thank God my grandmother is not in the room because she would have answered for me.

"What would you want me to say?" I finally ask. "I haven't done a speaking engagement in 10 years. I don't know if I have that in me anymore Momma."

"Just share your story and what you have accomplished so far," she said.

"I will think about this." I promised,

"Ok son, let me know if you change your mind." she said.

After we hang up, I sit on the couch in the sunroom in deep thought. The last speaking engagement I did was 2004-2005. A speech and debate competition. That was 13 years ago!

What would I say? How many people were going to be attending this workshop?

Suddenly, my mind is racing.

No pressure.

Even though Momma Hallback is not pressuring me to say yes, I should say yes.

This skill took places years ago, you met so many amazing people and had some amazing experiences. I remind myself. *This is an opportunity to do things differently this time around. Call Her Back.*

"Momma Hallback, I will do it."

We chat a little more and then we hang up.

I put the date into my phone and writer in my planner, then go back to reading my book because it calms me down. I have 3 weeks before October 10th arrives.

No Pressure.

October 10th arrives before I could even blink. The only form of preparation I did was I watched a recording of myself on my Instagram Page reciting the poem, "Be The Best of Whatever You Are" by Douglas Malloch.

I am about to walk into a speaking engagement with no notes. What the Hell am I thinking?

This is not what a great speaker does. A great speaker would do his due diligence and prepare. If I were an actor, would I show up to set and not remember my lines?

Too late to turn back now.

The venue is a church in Miami Gardens. I hug Momma Hallback as she is setting up and then people start to arrive.

Showtime.

I take my seat in front of Momma Hallback. My grandmother is seated in the back of the room. That is her way of making sure that I do not make eye contact with her while I am on stage.

I take a look at the agenda and notice I am supposed to speak the last 15 minutes of the workshop. I scan the crowd, so far only 13 people have shown up. That's great. These people don't know me, they don't know my story.

Each passing moment builds up anticipation. I am a little nervous because I still don't know what I am going to say.

Then I hear Momma Hallback. She is talking about her vocational path and all the different positions that she held over the years and at that moment, something clicked.

At this point in my life, I was intrigued by the idea of entrepreneurship and I wanted to work for myself in some form. That's when I came up with an idea.

Share your path to entrepreneurship. What if sharing your journey inspires someone? I thought.

About 45 minutes later, Momma Hallback introduces me and tells the crowd who I am and how our phone conversations start off. A little Spanish gibberish.

I start off with that, and the crowd starts laughing as I take the stage. Excellent icebreaker. It definitely relaxes me.

So, I share my path to entrepreneurship. The 15 minutes flew by! Everyone was laughing and smiling. Looking at the crowd's facial expressions reminded me of the speaking back in the day. How excited everyone was to hear me speak.

At the end of the event, Momma Hallback and I spoke with a few people who attended the workshop and they expressed what a great job we had done.

By the end of the event, I realized two things: One, I still had the gift of gab, and two, I missed public speaking. Sometimes, we have to let things go in order for us to realize how much we missed them.

CHAPTER 16

Back in 2010, I was introduced to the industry of Direct Sales/Network Marketing. That "thing" that your brother, sister, or best friend calls you up about and invites you to a presentation to hear about their products and opportunity.

Now, before you jump to the wrong conclusion, hear me out.

The Network Marketing industry is not as bad as you think. Yes, there are some people out there not building businesses with integrity.

But there are also legit companies with great products, and great people.

I used the industry to build relationships. I met some awesome people who have become life-long friends and partners outside of the industry.

One of them is Tom Crow. I connected him in 2017. He was still working in Information Technology while building his Network Marketing Business on the side.

I knew from our chats that Tom was someone I wanted to work with. He is open-minded, creative, down-to-earth, and has a great sense of humor. He is also very passionate about entrepreneurship.

One evening while chatting with him, we realized we were not happy professionally. He was looking to change careers from IT, and I was looking to start my career as a writer. And while we had the vehicle of networking marketing, it had become exhausting and we no longer had passion for it.

So, I offered Tom the opportunity to collaborate with me on a story that I had written a few years back. He was open to the idea because it was something he had never done. While some people would have been scared, Tom was fired up and I loved his energy because I was fired up.

We started developing a concept for a character and a storyline around his career in IT.

I kid you not, from 2017-2019, Tom and I must have written and rewritten at least 20 different drafts of our concept. But here is another reason why Tom and I are friends. When he commits to something, he is all in.

You need people like that in life and in business because those people will keep the fire burning on days when you don't feel like it.

LESSON 8: Entrepreneurship is a Rollercoaster

If you have not read the book "The Entrepreneurial Roller Coaster," by Darren Hardy I recommend that you do because no truer words have been spoken.

Entrepreneurship is a rollercoaster! And anyone that tells you it's not, is lying their ass off!

One day you are flourishing! I mean you are unstoppable. You are building your brand, you are making connections, you are getting opportunities to make money, and the next day, you plummet down that drop and your emotions are all over the place.

Suddenly you find yourself questioning EVERYTHING!

Why did I decide to do this?

What is my purpose?

How am I going to make this work?

Why is it not happening fast enough for me?

What's my next move if this doesn't work?

These are all the questions I was asking myself in the middle of 2019 because for about 3-4 months, NOTHING was working for me. I had no energy to create. I was upset and I didn't talk to anyone about how I was feeling, not my family, not my friends.

I had to figure this out on my own.

I read an article that said when a writer is creating characters, they should conduct an interview with that character.

So, in order to get my emotions in check, I would talk to myself in front of the mirror almost as if I were interviewing a character in one of my shows.

Sometimes you need to do this. You have to let out these emotions. Dance to your favorite music, or have yourself a good cry. Let it out because here is another thing, no one tells you about entrepreneurship:

This emotional rollercoaster is part of the process. It is a part of your growth. How you respond to this adversity will determine your success.

As 2019 progressed, so did my skill set.

One day, I received a phone call from one of my grandfather's friends. His wife, actually. She was a nervous wreck. She was in school earning her nursing degree and needed help writing a research paper in APA style.

Luckily for her, APA Style was all I wrote in college. So, I agreed to help her.

We met almost every day for 2-3 weeks helping her with formatting, in-text citations, references. She ended up getting an A on the paper.

After receiving her grade, she asked me, "How much do I owe you?"

I was shocked.

I didn't really think about this skill as something I could use to make extra money. But I was willing to give it a try because I knew what my goals were.

A few months later, I received a call from my Godbrother Braxton. He is a successful author with his own publishing company in Atlanta. He had seen a post that I had put on Instagram offering my editing services to college students.

He offered me an opportunity to be an editor on his team and I greatly accepted.

Not only was this my first job in entertainment, this was an opportunity to learn from someone with a production company.

Here is something I learned about Braxton. One, he started writing at 35 years old, and two, his academic background has NOTHING to do with TV, acting, or writing. He is a physical therapist.

He is still a practicing physical therapist which means, he still works a job while building his creative empire.

I know you are probably thinking, "How does a physical therapist break into entrepreneurship? How does one find the time?

Refer back to Lesson 6: Make a Decision and Start!

<u>CHAPTER 17</u>

March 9, 2020

I am at a friend's house discussing the possibility of working alongside her on a project. As we are talking, I glance up at the TV and I see the crawl at the bottom of the screen. Two major events in Miami had just been canceled, The Miami Dade Youth Fair, and The Calle Ocho festival as safety precaution because the number of COVID cases were on the rise.

A couple days later, Miami was on lockdown. Suddenly, the magic city that was always hustling and bustling with tourists was a ghost town. Everyone was told to stay home.

Now as an introvert, the first couple days and weeks were heaven. I had time to reflect and get to work on some projects that I had been putting off.

But that small moment of relief quickly changed a few weeks later.

My mom called and told me that my grandmother Helen was being admitted to the hospital.

I am extremely blessed because I have my grandparents and my great-grandparents on both sides of my family. My grandmother Helen is my Mom's mother but we were both raised by great-grandmother Catherine.

My grandmother Helen suffered a stroke 10 years ago, and since then she fought like hell. That's the thing about my family, we are strong-willed.

Grandma Helen passed away in April of 2020. It was devastating for my mom, my great-grandmother Catherine, and for me. My biggest regret is that I did not spend as much time with her as I should have, but I knew that she loved me and I loved her.

I lost two other relatives within 3 months of my grandmother's passing.

As 2020 progressed, something clicked off in my mind. It something that my mom always tells me:

"You have got to live your life. Whatever you want to do in this life, put your best foot forward and do it! Don't let nothing or no one stop you."

The reason this message was so clear to me now was because 2020 was filled with so much loss, and uncertainty for many families across the U.S. I am sure that those people prior to the pandemic had goals and dreams they wanted to achieve.

At that moment, I knew I could not wait any longer to pursue my dreams. I had to act.

Fast forward to 2021, the world had started to open back up so I got to work. I registered RGT Media Productions with the state of Florida.

I was excited because I had taken the first step in becoming a writer and a producer.

But that excitement quickly triggered my anxiety. Here we are back again on this emotional rollercoaster of Entrepreneurship.

Remember, that roller coaster is filled with ups, downs, twists, and turns.

Now the questions swirling around in my head are something like this:

"What did I just do?"

"Do I really have enough experience to do this?"

My stomach is in knots, my chest is beating fast. I am second guessing my decision.

This rollercoaster is about to get a lot worse.

A few nights later, I am sitting on the couch watching TV and I don't feel my best. I feel like an elephant is sitting on my chest and refusing to move. Then, I become nauseous. This is not me overthinking a decision. This is something else.

I listen to my body when it sends me signs. If something doesn't feel right, I am going to get checked out.

Good thing I did because after running an EKG, the doctor determined I had a very small arrhythmia, which I already knew.

But what the doctor told me next shocked me.

"Do you take Vitamin D Supplements?

"Yes, I do," I responded.

"How much?" he asked.

"5,000 IU's," I said.

"A day?" she said, raising an eyebrow. That's too much. You might have overdosed."

You can overdose on Vitamin D Supplements? Who Knew!

The reason I am sharing this part of my story is because it is something that Entrepreneurs often overlook. Some of us get so caught up in achieving success that we sacrifice our wellness for success.

If your mental and physical health are not a priority, your business will suffer.

Go for your checks-ups, schedule those appointments for your annual exams. Exercise and eat the right foods.

Your health is your greatest asset.

CHAPTER 18

When I was 18, my mom and I got into a heated argument over the phone about some documents I needed for school. My grandparents and I had been trying to call her for several days and she would not pick up the phone. When I finally did reach her, I gave her a piece of my mind. I don't remember every word we said, but I do remember the last thing I said to her when she finally let me speak:

"You know Mom, if you want to be my mother, and be in my life, great! If you don't, then that's on you! I will be just fine."

Click.

After that conversation, I did not talk to my mom for six months. It was the first time I stood up for myself. I was not going to call her back and apologize, nor was I going to take back what I said. I tolerated the disrespect because I was a kid and I didn't have any control over the situation. It was an uncomfortable, but necessary, conversation.

It's part of Knowing Your Worth!

LESSON 9: KNOW YOUR WORTH

Knowing Your Worth goes so much deeper than money. It is also about how people treat you. Here is an example.

Back in 2021, I took a position as a project manager with a startup non-profit. Although it wasn't the most exciting opportunity, it was a path that would help me build connections and possibly get me back to public speaking.

One night as I'm laying on the couch, the president of the organization calls me and asks me to look over a draft of a press release. I'd only been working with the organization a few days and I guess she thought I was new to working so I would be okay with being on call at 1:30 a.m.

Strike One.

A few days later, we are to meet with the city of Medley. On the way over, she instructs me, "if the mayor asks you any questions, you don't respond."

"Okay…?" I follow up with, *"So, just stand there and look. Got it!"*

Strike Two!

The Final strike came a few days after that. The president had given me a list of organizations to call and set up some meetings. After following up with a few of them over the course of a week and no responses back, I told the president that this wasn't working.

"You are wasting time going over that list. We have to move to the next task. We can't waste time. The mayor wants this project completed already."

"No, this is not going to work for me," I said.

"Excuse me?" she said.

"You need to find someone else that can work at your pace." I said. "Good luck, and I wish you the best."

I resigned after only two weeks on the job. Here's why:

    1. She had no strategy or plan in place.
    2. She had no respect for someone else's time.
    3. She could not complete a task before she moved on to the next thing.
    4. She didn't like to listen to people under her.

All of that made that experience extremely toxic. But there was one more element that also sealed the deal for my resignation.

She did not want to pay me what I was worth.

Keep in mind, that this is someone who knew me since I was eight years old. She knew my skill set and what I could bring to her organization.

I know some of you are thinking, "Forget about your worth, shut up and go to work!"

No! Absolutely not, and here's why: your worth is non-negotiable.

This is not your grandparents' economy where you have to stay on a job for 30-40 years and be overworked, underpaid, and underappreciated.

There is nothing wrong with having a job if that job is paying you a decent living wage, or if you enjoy what it is that you do because there are some people that love to work.

There is nothing wrong with having a job if you have no income, no experience, and no skill to help you make money. Then by all means, take that job, and learn everything you can.

However, if that job is not aligned with your goals and where you are trying to go, if that job is not paying you a decent wage, if your supervisors are treating you like crap, LEAVE!
Staying at a dead-end job is like staying in a relationship where you are not happy because you think there is no other option.

Refer to Lessons 5, 6, and 7.

Friends, know your worth, stand up for yourself, and what you believe in.

Both experiences taught me that not everyone is going to make it into your future. You have to let people go in order to make room for the new people that appreciate you, that value you.

Having uncomfortable conversations is scary, but necessary, in order to get people to respect you. You have to know when to draw the line with disrespect. You have to know when to say enough is enough.

That uncomfortable conversation with my mom has made our relationship a million times better. She now knows what I will stand for and what I won't. But if I hadn't, where would our relationship be as mother and son?

People only treat you one way: How you allow them to treat you.

Know that you are worth respect. Put a price on it and then add more!

CHAPTER 19

There is an old saying:

"When someone you haven't heard from in a while crosses your mind, check on them. God did that for a reason."

In August of 2021, I was scrolling through my Facebook friends and I stumbled upon the profile of someone I had not spoken to in 5 years.

It was Daniel Block, who I connected with in 2013. We were both a part of a network marketing company and we hit it off. But, we lost touch.

The last time I spoke with Dan, he was the owner and operator of his own gym. Now as we were messaging each other on Facebook, I learned that he made the transition into real estate.

I told him I was aggressively pursuing my writing, acting, and producing career and as we continued talking, I shared a short piece of a script I had written back in college. Then my creative brain shifted into gear.

Looking at his profile picture, he definitely looked like he could be an actor. Six feet tall, Caucasian, blonde hair, athletic. Definitely the type of guy that a casting director would discover in a coffee shop.

Without even thinking about it, I insert this into the conversation.

"Don't take this the wrong way but, as I am re-writing this script, I thought about you."

"Haha, I won't take it the wrong way, I am sure it's an adventure. I will let you know if anything like this happens for me," he replied.

"I mean, I want to pay you to play one of the roles," I said.

"Hell Yeah! That sounds great. I am always thinking that would be fun! Lemme know more," he replied.

Although I was directionless about my path and my purpose, I was always drawn to telling stories. Sometimes we have to take a detour from our original path, go down a different road to get back to where we want to go.

Daniel and I continued talking for the next few weeks. By our third conversation, I had already revised that short piece into a 10-page script. Daniel and I began meeting every week on his lunch break to read lines.

As we are reading, I noticed something about Dan's delivery.

It doesn't sound forced; he doesn't sound like an amateur. Everything about his delivery is natural.

"Have you done this before?" I asked.

"The only acting experience I have is, from a commercial when I was 7."

We both laugh. But part of me thinks, "This is crazy!" and the other part of me thinks, "This could be really fun!"

Dan then asked me, "What are your plans for this? How many scenes?

"There are at least 4. We could film this in a weekend. As far as time, would the end of next year work better or next summer sometime?" I responded.

"The timing doesn't need to be that far off," he said. "But I would like to know more about the project in general. Is it a short film?"

"It's a short film," I responded. "When would you like to get started?"

"Just depends on life, but if we planned on it a few months out, it shouldn't be a problem," he said.

Now it was time to get busy!

LESSON 9: SUCCESS LOVES SPEED

There is a motivational speech by Steve Harvey on YouTube called "JUMP!" Go to YouTube and watch it! It is Amazing.

The message? If you want to achieve success, you have to Jump!

You see, success loves speed and if you want to achieve success, you can't sit around and wait for an opportunity to be given to you. You can't sit around and overthink every part of the process. YOU HAVE TO JUMP!

Dan and I re-connected in August of 2021. By September of 2021, I had written five, fifteen-minute episodes. My short film concept evolved into a web series with more characters and a deeper storyline.

For those six weeks I was writing, I was focused. I have a huge realization: First, I was not overthinking every little detail of the process like I did before and two, for the first time since I started writing, I completed a script from start to finish, which meant momentum was being created and it felt great.

For the first time in a while, I feel happy, I feel at peace. I am proud of myself.

But here's the thing with momentum, you can lose speed if you are easily distracted.

For example, you are writing your screenplay or your book, but suddenly, you are distracted because your best friend rings your doorbell with wine, or your family is crashing at your house for 4 days, or a marathon of your favorite TV show is on.

Don't get it twisted, we all need a break. Spend time with your friends and family. Celebrate these milestones in your business.

What I am saying is develop a routine and stay on track. Your success and the speed at which you achieve your goals is dependent on your routine and how committed you are.

CHAPTER 20

January 8, 2022

Dan arrived at my house from California and we shot a few scenes of the script using my iPhone camera.

I am a nervous wreck!

Nervous because:

1. This is my company's first project
2. This is my first acting gig as well as Dan's first acting gig.
3. This is my first time going public as a writer, actor, and producer, and going public with your goals, intentions, or your new business venture is SCARY!

Scary because people on social media can be cruel. So yes, I am nervous about the feedback!

The nerves quickly wash away when I realize how much fun I am having. Not just with filming and acting but re-connecting with Dan.

Social media is powerful. If utilized properly, the people you connect with can become some of the most honest, supportive, down-to-earth, friends for life.

I am having so much fun, I don't want the weekend to end.

Later that night, I am having a phone conversation with my sister-from-another-mister Tavahni Quaterman. She and I grew up attending the same church. Church of the Incarnation in Miami, Florida. Her mother's birthday is the day after mine, October 28th.

Tavahni and I re-connected in 2020. At the time, she was a police officer in Apopka, Florida. Growing up, that was her dream job. But suddenly, she was unfulfilled, burnt-out, looking for a change.

Sound familiar?

I told her about my production company, the project I was developing and offered her an opportunity to play one of the roles and she agreed!

Was she scared? Totally!

But she tried it because she wanted to learn something new and she wanted to support me.

Following that weekend, I posted the scenes we shot to Facebook and Instagram. The feedback was well received.

Now that I had gone public, I could not stop. I had to keep going. I had an audience!

Remember Lesson 9: Success Loves Speed. Continue to build momentum.

Now I had to put my thinking cap on because I needed to build my team. I needed a crew and five other actors.

I am officially on a New Rollercoaster: The Rollercoaster of Experience!

I did not have any actor or actress friends in the industry on speed dial whom I could offer these roles to. Most of my classmates and friends had jobs. I could feel myself starting to lose that momentum as the overthinking re-appeared.

My emotions will not get the better of me this time. *I can do this!* I There are people out there looking for work. I reached out to some of my contacts and was referred to Andrew "AJ" Perez, a Miami based photographer and videographer.

During my first meeting with him, we discussed the story, production timeline, process, shots, editing. Then, he asked me an important question.

"Based on everything we have discussed; how much do you think this will cost?"

I have already made a few assumptions. The first is that this production would cost at least $50,000 and two, to hire Andrew is going cost me at least $10,000.

I knew from my research that the average cost to produce a TV show can range anywhere from $100,000 to $1 million an episode.

When Andrew hears the number, his eyes widen with surprise. "We can make this look great for waaay less," he said.

Universe? Is this really happening?

So, we agree on a number that is do-able for the entire first season.

We kicked production off in May of 2022. That weekend, we shot 5 scenes in 6 hours. One videographer, 3 actors.

Teamwork

I still needed three actors to play the roles in upcoming scenes. Our next shoot date was a few weeks away. I turned to social media. I wrote out the character descriptions and posted them to my social pages.

I didn't expect one post to solve my problem. I had to network! I look at the character breakdown list, and the character of Malcolm jumps out at me.

The character breakdown of Malcolm was as follows:

Sergeant Malcolm Maddox (40's) African American, Street Smart. Protective Father to his son AJ whom he loves dearly. Dedicated and respected cop who will bend the rules to protect the people he loves.

Thanks to Instagram and its algorithm, I knew someone. Shaun Grant.

You see, Instagram has this thing it does where someone will randomly begin following you. Normally they will like maybe one or two photos and then they will be gone in a day or two. Shaun, however, stayed.

I reached out to him on Instagram and asked would be interested in the role of Malcolm. I sent him the script, and after reading it, he accepted, to my relief.

A few weeks later, my phone rings. It's Marc Jacir. It's been a minute since I have spoken to him. We chat for a little bit and then he asks me what I have been up to. I tell him about the series I am producing and he is intrigued.

I send him the script; he reads over a few days and then we chat again. He asks me what roles are left and I tell him about the character of Silas Redding.
Marc and I start talking about how we can develop Silas into a badass character.

Marc tells me about his time in the finance industry and why he walked away from it. By the end of the conversation, the character of Silas went from good to great! Suddenly Silas had mystery, intrigue, purpose, emotion. When you develop a character with those elements, the writing process becomes so much fun.

I knew this was the beginning of something great!

LESSON 10: BUILD YOUR TEAM

I listened to an interview by Issa Rae, the creator of the TV series *Insecure*. In the interview, she talked about networking and how we should use the people around us.

"Who's next to you?

"Who needs an opportunity?

"Who is willing to try something new?"

"Who is willing to take the journey with you regardless of the outcome?"
Find those people and get to work

I had already experienced this by bringing on Dan, Andrew, Tavahni, Marc, Shaun, and Tom. These were the people next to me, in the trenches with me, and hungry to see me succeed. But there were still people missing.

By the time we began shooting scenes for the second episode of the series, I still did not have all the actors I needed. I messaged Shaun Grant one evening and asked him if he could help me find a few people.

Boy, did he deliver!

I woke up the next morning and my inbox was flooded with emails from actors and actresses all over Florida, wanting to audition for roles!

I have heard some people say that success is lonely at the top because you can't bring everyone with you.

To some people, success means being able to do it all yourself.

To me, that is not a vibe that I subscribe to!

Don't get me wrong, in the beginning you will wear multiple hats in your business. Eventually though, you will need a team! As you build and expand, you will discover that there are tasks when it comes to running a business that you don't like or aren't using your gift.

For example, when it comes to social media management, I am not an expert. But I do have someone; Megan Block and she is Amazing!!

Success does not have to be lonely at the top if you have the right people around you that want to see you succeed. Find your people, be good to them, and watch your business flourish!

CHAPTER 21

Six months into 2022. My series officially has a name, "The Associates." People are curious, including my grandmother Marie. A few days after we finished filming scenes from the second episode, she asked me a question.

"What are you guys doing?"

"We are filming a TV show." I said.

"A TV show?" she said, raising a curious eyebrow.

"Yes, like FBI, and Chicago PD." I responded.

"What is your role in all of this?"

"I wrote it, I am producing it, and acting in it."

She stood still, trying to process this conversation, mind spinning. You have to understand, for years she wanted me to do something, ANYTHING in television, and I would not budge!

I wished I could tell her more about the process, but I can't because I am a firm believer in this rule: **Do let them know what you are doing until it's done.**

As we progress through 2022, I slowly feel that momentum fading again. Not that I am doubting myself or overthinking, but something is missing. Now let me clear, I was not lacking creative projects. I have at least 5 projects on my computer that I needed to finish.

I love writing, I love to tell stories.

But something has come over me. A desire of sorts. A desire to motivate, inspire, to teach!

I can't believe I just said that out loud.

As I said in the beginning of this journey, my grandmother Marie was an educator for 40 years! Some of my grandparent's best friends were educators, and some of my grandmother's cousins were educators.

You would think by me being surrounded by a long line of dedicated educators that I would follow in their footsteps, right?

Wrong! It is scary being a teacher in America. Look at everything they have to deal with:

1. Low pay
2. No support from Administration
3. School safety

These are some of the main reasons teachers across America are leaving the profession. Knowing all of this, I asked myself. "Why would I even want to entertain becoming a teacher?"

I headed back to St. Thomas University to visit Dr Knowles. It's been a few months since I have seen her.

"You know Ray, I've told you before, you are too much of an intellectual not to continue your PhD. You are still young. Give it time."

The idea is definitely buried somewhere deep inside me. Maybe, I will say yes to that challenge.

Maybe.

CHAPTER 22

I used to hear my grandmothers, Mattie and Marie, say the following:

"You have got to see and be seen."

In other words, success is all about seizing opportunities, and being in the right place at the right time.

One Sunday in December 2022, I am in church, setting up the livestream for church service, a young man approaches me and introduces himself. His name is Gardy.

I had heard "of" Gardy through my friend, Reverend James Bell, but assumed that Gardy was older. To my surprise, Gardy was younger than me.

Anyway, we strike up a conversation. I shared a little about myself and my journey into becoming a writer and a producer and he is amazed.

"Have you heard of Voyage Magazine?" he asked.

"Yes, I have," I responded.

Voyage Magazine is an online publication that highlights local artists, and entrepreneurs. Several acquaintances had been featured there.

"Would you be interested in being featured?" he asked.

"Yes, I would love that," I said.

Wow! Talk about growth! I am proud of myself, because the guy from 10 years ago, the guy who slammed the door on his God-Given-Gift of public speaking, was now saying yes to an opportunity for exposure.

If you want people to know who you are, what you are doing, and if you want your friends and family to stop asking you, "What are you doing with yourself now?" You have to start and build your momentum.

Whether it is an opportunity to speak at an event, an opportunity to sell your product, an opportunity to be featured on a magazine, or podcast, or interviewed on someone's YouTube Channel. Take it!

Don't worry if they talk about you. They are going to talk regardless! Stay focused on your goals. Give the world something to talk about!

About 3 weeks later, I received an email from Voyage Magazine asking if I would be interested in being featured. Suddenly, this feeling washed over me. A feeling of excitement.

Thank God I did not give up on my dreams!

The excitement quickly turns into anxiety as I read the e-mail and discover I have 2 weeks to put this article together. They need at least 5-8 images of me.

HOLY CRAP!

I call my mom and share with her the good news! I hear my great-grandmother Catherine in the background. If my great-grandmother hears about this, she is going to shout it from the mountain tops.

Now don't get me wrong, it is a great thing when your friends and family celebrate your success because they believe in you and love you. However, the element of surprise is gone!

Think about when you were a kid and how you looked forward to Christmas. There was an element of surprise, spending days and weeks wondering if you would get what you asked for.

My point is, when it comes to success, people believe that being successful means sharing every detail of your process to social media before the goal takes flight. Yes, you can have successful people around you that truly want to see you succeed, but that does not mean everyone will.

As I said earlier, the envy around success is real. Often, the envy comes from people who:

1. Have never done what you are trying to do.
2. Had a bad experience attempting to achieve a goal
3. Received guidance from the wrong person.

These are the people who will try to plant a seed of doubt in your head. If you allow people to project their fears onto you, you will be back on that roller coaster of emotion, questioning everything. Let there be an element of surprise to your success.

CHAPTER 23

We have now come full circle. The Voyage Miami article went live January 12, 2023, and my family went nuts! Suddenly everyone was curious about what I was doing.

Three days later, my team and I were filming the next leg of scenes for The Associates and for the first time since we began shooting, I ran into a problem! An actor whom I had hired had gone radio silent. As people were arriving to begin shooting for the day, I got a text message saying in not so many words, "Thanks for the opportunity, you should seek someone else."

Not exactly what I wanted to hear at the moment.

I had gone through so many hoops in the days and weeks leading up to January 15th, there was no way I was going to tell the 7 people who made the effort to show up, that filming was canceled.

Come on...think!

As if God himself heard my dilemma, the answer to my problem was a few steps away from me. One of the actresses had made the drive down to Miami with her boyfriend. I used him in the other actor's place.

Problem solved!

As we were filming that day, a neighbor two doors down from me saw us shooting a scene and called me over in between takes.

"Hey, sweetheart, what is going on over there?"

"We are filming a TV show, Miss Joyce," I responded.

Her eyes widened with excitement. "If you ever need an extra, call me!"

We both laughed but I knew she is very serious. I went back to work.

LESSON 11: IMPROVISE

There will come a time when you have to improvise. You will have to change your strategy or your plan sometimes at the last minute.

When I first began production with "The Associates," two of the scenes required two different locations. I was able to find both of them, however, one location was only available during the week, and the other would have taken money out of the budget.

So I used my backyard for one scene and my living room for the other.

Use the resources and people you have available and improvise! Improvisation encourages creativity and forces you to think on your feet.

Your ability to solve problems quickly can mean the difference between a successful shooting day or a complete disaster.

What would have become of "The Associates" if I gave up at the first sign of adversity? It would still be just an idea in my head. I would find ways to sabotage my success. I would once again be on that emotional rollercoaster questioning everything.

Be a problem solver. Improvise. But most importantly, never give up!

CHAPTER 24

June 24, 2012

I am getting dressed in a gold shirt and black suit for my grandparent's George and Marie's 50th wedding anniversary. It was beautiful! Being surrounded by family and close friends to see two people who truly love each other make it to 50 years is beautiful!

I cried my eyes out standing up there with them because I was happy because they have been through a lot together. Especially my grandfather George who still fights every day to live despite the health issues he has faced and is still facing.

Why am I taking you back to this moment?

Because of a question that I am sure many of you get often just as I do.

When are you going to find a "significant other?"

Here's the thing. My grandparents George and Marie have been married for 60 years. My great grandparents Catherine and Jessie have been married for 70 years. My Uncle Todd and his wife have been married for 26 years and have two beautiful children. I know that love exists. They are living proof.

Do I believe there is someone out there for everyone? Absolutely!

I love that two people can come together, build a life, and be happy. Happiness is needed in this crazy world.

However, for me, at least at this stage in my life, *I do not want a significant other. At least not in the traditional way.*

My Godfather Johnny Stepherson is a perfect example of what I am talking about. He was married 34 years to his wife Connie before she passed away in 2004. Now, he has an amazing woman in his life, Priscilla. But, they are not married. It is a beautiful companionship meaning, they don't need each other for financial support, and they each have their own homes. When they come together, they have a great time. They go to parties, dinner, lunch, social functions, and at the end of the day, they go their separate ways. I love that.

I love the freedom that being single provides me. I am not saying I would make a horrible boyfriend, husband, or father, I'm saying for me, being able to go out, and come back without being questioned is priceless.

I suppose I have my younger years to thank for this. I did not do much socializing as a kid. I was an introverted/extrovert. I didn't have a best friend until high school. But overall, it taught me an important lesson: Learn to be happy with yourself first, before you can be happy with someone else.

Finding companionship is a work in progress which I will not allow to impede progress. That is what can happen with a relationship at the wrong time in your life.

Imagine you are a writer sitting at your laptop working. Headphones in your ear, in deep thought to the point where everything around you is non-existent.

Suddenly you hear your "significant other" shout from the bedroom,
"Babe, are you coming?

Without taking your eyes off the screen and still typing, you yell back,

"Yeah, be right there babe."

So you stop writing in order to have quality time. Nothing wrong with that at all, but ask yourself. ***What are you willing to give up in order to achieve your goals?***

As a writer, it is an art form that requires discipline and sacrifice. As a writer, you will get spontaneous inspiration late at night while in bed, and not everyone will understand this deep-rooted connection you have with creativity.

I have sacrificed A LOT to get here. Dinners, parties with family and friends, vacations, you name it.

All I am saying is take your time with this phase in your life. Do not let anyone pressure you with their timelines.

There are some people who spend so much time comparing themselves to others.

We spend our lives believing we have to follow the same path our parents took. Go To College. Graduate. Get a Job. Get Married. Have kids. Work. Retire.

We believe that if we do not follow this path, that we have somehow let them down or defied their expectations of us.

That my friends is exhausting!

Follow your heart! Create your own path.

You want to transition from your 9-5 job to become an actor or writer full time? Great! Put a plan in place and get to work and work your tail off every single day!

You don't want to get married? Don't.

You wanna go to trade or vocational school instead of college? Go ahead! There are people out there without college degrees making money!

There is more than one way to achieve success, friends. Flip the script, change the narrative. It is okay!

CHAPTER 25

I am sitting on the edge of my grandmother's Marie bed looking through the old scrapbooks. I realize I have come a long way! I have made some incredible memories with some incredible people.

I stumble upon a speech that I had made for the Children's Home Society Graduating class in 2003 and the speech goes like this:

Good afternoon Ladies and Gentleman, and to you the graduating class. Wow!! What a pleasure to be here this afternoon! I am really happy that I was invited to participate and help celebrate this year's graduating class of 2002. You all look great boys and girls. I was having a conversation with my grandmother on the way here this afternoon and as usual she was explaining to me the importance of having respect for others, to be loving, always have a good attitude, and most of all to believe in yourself. If you believe in yourself, the sky's the limit. Believe that you deserve to be loved, believe that you deserve success. Believe that you can achieve anything you set your mind to. Even if you encounter obstacles, learn from them, grow, and keep going. Yes, you can and yes you will succeed. The future is yours! Good luck and congratulations.

Twenty years later and that message still remains the same. You have to Believe in Yourself. My journey here was full of adversity. It took a village, it took discipline, it took belief in myself and my abilities.

If someone told me 13 years ago, that I would be here today, I would not have believed them. Yet here I am…

A Survivor
A better son
A Better Grandson
A loyal friend
An Entrepreneur
A strong Leader
A Writer

Someone who is willing to take more chances on himself to get to the next level.

Looking at all the photos, I love who I have become. That baby that was medically declared dead who turned into the little boy who kids were cruel to. He sees the person I've become and he loves it.

The young man who was Young, Gifted, and Directionless in college, I have forgiven for his shortcomings. It's all good! My journey is just beginning.

I cannot wait to see where this journey leads in the next 20 years. I know it will be amazing!

So my friends, whatever it is you are trying to accomplish, believe in yourself.

Forgive yourself.

Love who you are!

Trust the process and enjoy the journey!

You've got this! I believe in You!

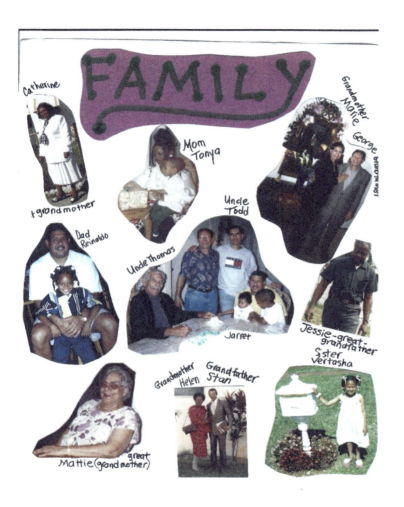

Family

Great Eggs !!!

One year old !!

Long wait !!

Ho
H
Ho

Not
Soo
Happy!

Not soo happy.....

Tips from the PRO, my Dad !!! ☺

Childhood Memories

Fun
Time!
Am I cute
or what!!

First bike!!!

On a roll.... 😊

On the job training!

First
Halloween !!
Ha! Ha!

Childhood Memories

My home for the first six months of my life.

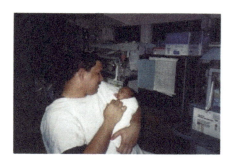

My dad came to visit me every day.

Sitting High

Delrish Moss and I, 2001. Wherever you saw me, you saw him.

First time giving a speech.

Nana and I with Jodi Atkinson, Executive Director of "Do The Right Thing" with Chief William O'Brien and members of the Miami PD, 1999.

Mom and I, 1998

Nana and I with Chief William O'Brien at the luncheon for "Do The Right Thing" before leaving to London, 1999.

Nana and I standing outside Royal National Hotel in London.

"Do the Right Thing" winners in Trafalgar Square.

Nana and I in Trafalgar Square. Look at the pigeons!!

I guess you can say I had a thing for podiums

Lt. Bill Schwartz and I.

Angel Calzadilla and I.

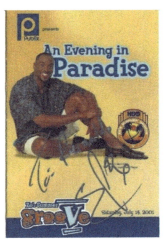

Autographed Program
Alonzo Mourning's
Summer Groove, 2001

Tommy and I at Zo's Summer Groove, 2001.

Jason Taylor of the Miami Dolphins at Zo's Summer Groove, 2001.

Charles Barkley and I at Zo's Summer Groove, 2001.

Jim Berry of CBS4 with Grandma Cat and I at Zo's Summer Groove, 2001

 Grandma Cat, Nana, and I at Zo's Summer Groove, 2001.

Jim Berry introducing me at Zo's Summer Groove, 2001.

Me giving the Invocational Prayer at Zo's Summer Groove, 2001.

Alonzo Mourning and I at Zo's Summer Groove, 2003.

Tracy Mourning and I in 2003.

Ma Josie and her kids at the Passover and Good Friday Service.

Josie's Six Pearls Masters of Ceremony for Passover and Good Friday Service.

Cafidia Stuart and I at "Showtime at the Apollo" audition.

Cafidia and I at a retirement celebration for Major Juanita Walker. Wherever you saw me, you saw her. When I spoke, she sang.

 Nana and I with Cousin Ingrid and Beverly at Justice Building Black History Program.

My Fifth Grade Drama Teacher, Michelle Riu.

Grandma Mattie and I

Cousin Pam, Grandma Cat, and I at Children's Home Society Graduation Luncheon, 2002.

Cousin Pam, Eduardo Diaz, and I at Children's Home Society Graduation Luncheon.

Nana, Grandma Cat, and I at Children's Home Society Dinner, 2003

Delrish and I in 2013 at Gun Buyback in Miami. I was intern for the Public Information Office my last semester of Undergrad.

Helping Sgt. Freddie Cruz give an interview, 2013.

Papi, Nana, and Grandma Cat. Masters Graduation 2017.

My high school best friend, Nick, and I.

Mom, Dad, and I at Master's graduation.

Delrish and I at his retirement from Miami PD in 2017.

Nana and I at Delrish's Retirement.

14 years of friendship in this photo. From high school to now!

Mama Hallback and I in 2018 at Vocational Workshop.

Frederica and I at her book signing in 2018.

Three generations of Torres Men.

Finally met Cousin Douglas, his son Daniel, and wife Theresa. He searched for his family for over 50 years.

Cousin Doug, Daniel, Theresa, Nana and I at Latin Grill.

My angels at Christmas.

Shaun Grant, Marc Jair, Daniel Block, and I after filming a scene of "The Associates."

Tom Crow, Shaun Grant, Steven Smith and I after filming a scene of the Associates.

Directing a scene with AJ Perez.

Candid shot in the middle of an intense scene as AJ Maddox.

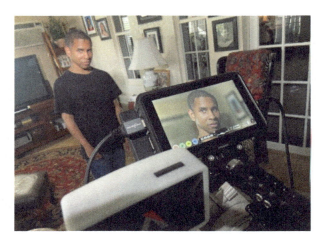

Getting ready to film!

I love who I am becoming.

About the Author

I am an entrepreneur born, raised, and still living in Miami Florida. I attended St Thomas University where I obtained my Bachelor's Degree in Communications in 2013, followed by a Masters in Management in 2017. I am CEO of RGT Media Productions and now I can add author to my list of accomplishments.

All you have to do is believe in yourself!!!!

Made in the USA
Monee, IL
29 June 2023

37899672R00077